MAKE A SW
pattern stitch, c
Make a beginnii
or larger swatch

M000233416

beginning chain. Crochet in your selected pattern until you have a square swatch.

MEASURE THE GAUGE. If you like your pattern stitch swatch, it's time to measure the gauge to determine the number of chains needed to design your project. Lay the swatch, right side up, on a flat, smooth surface. Measure the width of two full repeats of the multiple. Let's say two repeats measure 1". Now do the math.

Example: If two repeats of the multiple measure 1" and there are two chains in one multiple, you know it takes four chains to equal 1".

PLAN THE PROJECT. Decide what finished measurement you'd like, then figure how many chains are needed for the beginning chain.

Example: Using the 2 + 5 multiple again, let's say you are making a scarf with a finished measurement of 8" wide and your gauge is 2 repeats of the multiple per inch. Multiply 2 (repeats of the multiple) x 2 (stitches in one multiple) for a total of 4 chains. Then multiply 4 (chains) x 8 (width of project) for a total of 32 chains. You would then add 5 chains to equal 37, giving you a multiple of 2 + 5 chains. Work the pattern stitch to the desired length — just be sure to finish the row repeat.

Hint: Do not hesitate to add or subtract chains in order for your beginning chain to correspond with the multiple of your chosen pattern stitch.

Now that you have the basic guidelines for designing, choose a pattern stitch that sparks your imagination. Match it with that yarn you have been itching to use and let the sky be the limit!

PATTERN STITCHES

1. LATTICE
(Multiple of 2 + 1 ch)

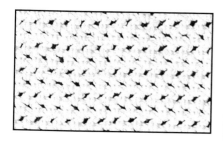

Ch 33 **loosely**.

Row 1 (Right side)**:** Hdc in fifth ch from hook, ★ ch 1, skip next ch, hdc in next ch; repeat from ★ across: 15 ch-sps.

Row 2: Ch 2 **(counts as first hdc, now and throughout)**, turn; hdc in first ch-sp, ★ ch 1, hdc in next ch-2 sp; repeat from ★ across, hdc in next ch: 14 ch-1 sps.

Row 3: Ch 3 **(counts as first hdc plus ch 1)**, turn; hdc in first ch-1 sp, ch 1, ★ hdc in next ch-1 sp, ch 1; repeat from ★ across, skip next hdc, hdc in last hdc: 15 ch-1 sps.

Row 4: Ch 2, turn; hdc in first ch-1 sp, ★ ch 1, hdc in next ch-1 sp; repeat from ★ across, hdc in last hdc: 14 ch-1 sps.

Repeat Rows 3 and 4 for pattern.

2. FAGGOT STITCH
(Multiple of 2 + 1 ch)

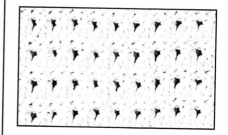

Ch 25 **loosely**.

Row 1: Sc in second ch from hook and in each ch across: 24 sc.

Row 2 (Right side)**:** Ch 2, turn; YO, insert hook in first sc, YO and pull up a loop, YO and draw through 2 loops on hook, (YO, insert hook in **next** sc, YO and pull up a loop, YO and draw through 2 loops on hook) twice, YO and draw through all 4 loops on hook, ch 2 **loosely**, ★ YO, insert hook in same sc as last st, YO and pull up a loop, YO and draw through 2 loops on hook, (YO, insert hook in **next** sc, YO and pull up a loop, YO and draw through 2 loops on hook) twice, YO and draw through all 4 loops on hook, ch 2 **loosely**; repeat from ★ across to last sc, hdc in last sc.

Row 3: Ch 1, turn; sc in first hdc and in next 2 chs, ★ skip next st, sc in next 2 chs; repeat from ★ across to last 2 sts, skip next st, sc in top of turning ch: 24 sc.

Repeat Rows 2 and 3 for pattern.

3. WEB
(Multiple of 13 + 4 chs)

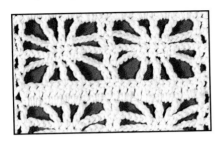

Ch 30 **loosely**.

Row 1: Dc in fourth ch from hook and in each ch across: 28 sts.

Row 2 (Right side): Ch 3, turn; dc in next dc and in each st across.

To work treble crochet (abbreviated tr), YO twice, insert hook in st indicated, YO and pull up a loop (4 loops on hook), (YO and draw through 2 loops on hook) 3 times *(Figs. 9a & b, page 22)*.

Row 3: Ch 3 **(counts as first dc, now and throughout),** turn; dc in next dc, ★ ch 5, (skip next 2 dc, tr in next dc) 3 times, ch 5, skip next 2 dc, dc in next 2 dc; repeat from ★ across.

Row 4: Ch 3, turn; dc in next dc, ★ ch 4, skip next 4 chs, sc in next ch, sc in next 3 tr and in next ch, ch 4, dc in next 2 dc; repeat from ★ across.

Row 5: Ch 3, turn; dc in next dc, ★ ch 5, skip next sc, sc in next 3 sc, ch 5, dc in next 2 dc; repeat from ★ across.

Row 6: Ch 3, turn; dc in next dc, ★ ch 2, (tr in next sc, ch 2) 3 times, dc in next 2 dc; repeat from ★ across.

Row 7: Ch 3, turn; dc in next dc, ★ 2 dc in next ch-2 sp, (dc in next tr, 2 dc in next ch-2 sp) 3 times, dc in next 2 dc; repeat from ★ across.

Repeat Rows 3-7 for pattern.

Last Row: Ch 3, turn; dc in next dc and in each dc across; finish off.

---

4. CROSSHATCH
(Multiple of 7 chs)

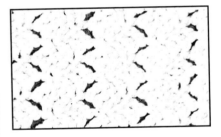

Ch 35 **loosely**.

Row 1: 2 Dc in third ch from hook, skip next 3 chs, sc in next ch, ★ ch 3, dc in next 3 chs, skip next 3 chs, sc in next ch; repeat from ★ across.

Row 2 (Right side): Ch 3, turn; 2 dc in first sc, ★ skip next 3 dc, sc in top of next ch-3, ch 3, dc in next 2 chs and in next sc; repeat from ★ across to last 3 sts, skip next 2 dc, sc in top of turning ch. Repeat Row 2 for pattern.

5. VERTICAL SCALLOP
(Multiple of 7 chs)

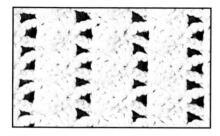

Ch 35 **loosely**.
Row 1: 3 Dc in fourth ch from hook, skip next 2 chs, sc in next ch, ★ ch 3, skip next 3 chs, 3 dc in next ch, skip next 2 chs, sc in next ch; repeat from ★ across.
Row 2 (Right side)**:** Ch 2, turn; 3 dc in first sc, ★ skip next 2 dc, sc in next dc, ch 3, 3 dc in next sc; repeat from ★ across to last 4 sts, skip next 3 dc, sc in top of turning ch.
Repeat Row 2 for pattern.

6. 3-DC SHELL STITCH
(Multiple of 4 chs)

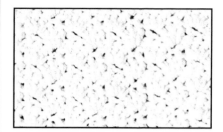

Ch 28 **loosely**.
Row 1 (Right side)**:** Dc in fourth ch from hook, skip next ch, sc in next ch, ★ skip next ch, 3 dc in next ch, skip next ch, sc in next ch; repeat from ★ across to last 2 chs, skip next ch, 2 dc in last ch.
Row 2: Ch 1, turn; sc in first dc, skip next dc, 3 dc in next sc, ★ skip next dc, sc in next dc, skip next dc, 3 dc in next sc; repeat from ★ across to last 2 sts, skip next dc, sc in top of turning ch.
Row 3: Ch 3, turn; dc in first sc, skip next dc, sc in next dc, ★ skip next dc, 3 dc in next sc, skip next dc, sc in next dc; repeat from ★ across to last 2 sts, skip next dc, 2 dc in last sc.
Repeat Rows 2 and 3 for pattern.

7. ACACIA STITCH
(Multiple of 5 + 1 ch)

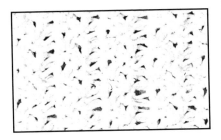

Ch 31 **loosely**.

Row 1 (Right side): Dc in fourth ch from hook, ★ sc in next ch, pull up loop on hook to measure ³/₄", skip next 3 chs, (dc, ch 1, dc) in next ch; repeat from ★ across to last 2 chs, skip next ch, sc in next ch.

Row 2: Ch 3, turn; skip first sc, dc in next dc, ★ sc in next ch-1 sp, pull up loop on hook to measure ³/₄", (dc, ch 1, dc) in next sc; repeat from ★ across to last 2 sts, skip next dc, sc in top of turning ch.

Repeat Row 2 for pattern.

8. SHADOW BOX
(Multiple of 11 + 4 chs)

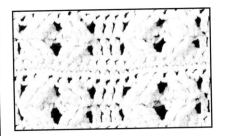

Ch 26 **loosely**.

Row 1: Sc in second ch from hook and in each ch across: 25 sc.

Rows 2 and 3: Ch 1, turn; sc in each st across.

To work treble crochet (abbreviated tr), YO twice, insert hook in st indicated, YO and pull up a loop (4 loops on hook), (YO and draw through 2 loops on hook) 3 times **(Figs. 9a & b, page 22)**.

Row 4 (Right side): Ch 3 **(counts as first dc)**, turn; dc in next 2 sts, ★ skip next 2 sts, tr in next 2 sts, working **behind** 2 tr just made, tr in 2 skipped sts, skip next 2 sts, tr in next 2 sts, working in **front** of 2 tr just made, tr in 2 skipped sts, dc in next 3 sts; repeat from ★ across.

Row 5: Repeat Row 4.

Repeat Rows 2-5 for pattern.

9. CROSSES
(Multiple of 11 + 4 chs)

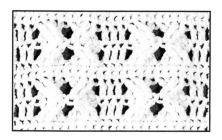

Ch 26 **loosely**.
Row 1 (Right side): Sc in second ch from hook and in each ch across: 25 sc.
Rows 2 and 3: Ch 1, turn; sc in each st across.
To work treble crochet (abbreviated tr), YO twice, insert hook in st indicated, YO and pull up a loop (4 loops on hook), (YO and draw through 2 loops on hook) 3 times *(Figs. 9a & b, page 22)*.
Rows 4 and 5: Ch 3 **(counts as first dc)**, turn; dc in next 2 sts, ★ skip next 2 sts, tr in next 2 sts, working **behind** 2 tr just made, tr in 2 skipped sts, skip next 2 sts, tr in next 2 sts, working in **front** of 2 tr just made, tr in 2 skipped sts, dc in next 3 sts; repeat from ★ across.
Repeat Rows 2-5 for pattern.

10. LACY V
(Multiple of 3 + 2 chs)

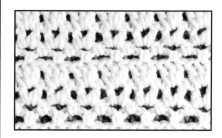

Ch 29 **loosely**.
Row 1: Dc in fifth ch from hook, ★ skip next 2 chs, (dc, ch 1, dc) in next ch; repeat from ★ across: 9 ch-sps.
Row 2 (Right side): Ch 3, turn; 2 dc in first ch-1 sp, 3 dc in each ch-sp across: 27 sts.
Row 3: Ch 1, turn; sc in first 2 dc, ★ ch 3, skip next 2 dc, sc in next dc; repeat from ★ across to last st, sc in top of turning ch: 8 ch-3 sps.
Row 4: Ch 1, turn; sc in first sc, ch 3, (sc in next ch-3 sp, ch 3) across, skip next sc, sc in last sc: 9 ch-3 sps.
Row 5: Ch 4, turn; dc in first ch-3 sp, (dc, ch 1, dc) in each ch-3 sp across.
Repeat Rows 2-5 for pattern.

11. BOW TIES
(Multiple of 13 + 1 ch)

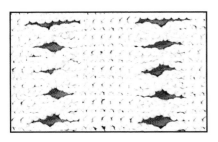

Ch 27 **loosely**.
Row 1 (Right side)**:** Sc in second ch from hook and in each ch across: 26 sc.
Row 2: Ch 1, turn; sc in first 3 sc, ch 8, skip next 7 sc, sc in next 6 sc, ch 8, skip next 7 sc, sc in last 3 sc.
Rows 3 and 4: Ch 1, turn; sc in first 3 sc, ch 8, sc in next 6 sc, ch 8, sc in last 3 sc.
Row 5: Ch 1, turn; sc in first 3 sc, ch 3, slip st around all three loops below, ch 3, sc in next 6 sc, ch 3, slip st around all three loops below, ch 3, sc in last 3 sc.
Row 6: Ch 1, turn; sc in first 3 sc, ch 8, sc in next 6 sc, ch 8, sc in last 3 sc.
Repeat Rows 3-6 for pattern, ending by working Row 5.
Next Row: Ch 1, turn; sc in first 3 sc, ch 7 **loosely**, sc in next 6 sc, ch 7 **loosely**, sc in last 3 sc.
Last Row: Ch 1, turn; sc in each sc and in each ch across; finish off: 26 sc.

12. GRANULE STITCH
(Multiple of 4 + 2 chs)

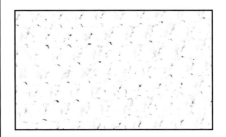

Ch 26 **loosely**.
Row 1: Sc in second ch from hook and in each ch across: 25 sc.
To work Picot sc, insert hook in st indicated, YO and pull up a loop, (YO and draw through 1 loop on hook) 3 times, YO and draw through both loops on hook.
Row 2 (Right side)**:** Ch 1, turn; sc in first sc, ★ work Picot sc in next sc, sc in next sc; repeat from ★ across.
Row 3: Ch 1, turn; sc in first sc and in each st across.
Row 4: Ch 1, turn; sc in first 2 sc, work Picot sc in next sc, (sc in next sc, work Picot sc in next sc) across to last 2 sc, sc in last 2 sc.
Row 5: Ch 1, turn; sc in first sc and in each st across.
Repeat Rows 2-5 for pattern.

13. DC DIAMONDS
(Multiple of 3 chs)

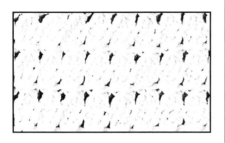

Ch 30 **loosely**.

Row 1: 3 Dc in fifth ch from hook, ★ skip next 2 chs, 3 dc in next ch; repeat from ★ across to last ch, dc in last ch.

Row 2 (Right side)**:** Ch 3, turn; ★ (YO, insert hook in **next** dc, YO and pull up a loop, YO and draw through 2 loops on hook) 3 times, YO and draw through all 4 loops on hook, ch 1; repeat from ★ across, dc in top of turning ch.

Row 3: Ch 3, turn; 3 dc in each ch-1 across, dc in top of turning ch.

Repeat Rows 2 and 3 for pattern.

14. DIAGONAL FENCE
(Multiple of 8 + 6 chs)

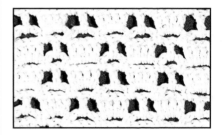

Ch 30 **loosely**.

Row 1: Sc in second ch from hook, ★ ch 3, skip next 3 chs, sc in next ch; repeat from ★ across: 7 ch-3 sps.

Row 2 (Right side)**:** Ch 3, turn; 4 dc in first ch-3 sp, ★ ch 1, dc in next ch-3 sp, ch 1, 4 dc in next ch-3 sp; repeat from ★ across, dc in last sc: 21 sts.

Row 3: Ch 1, turn; sc in first dc, ch 3, ★ sc in next ch-1 sp, ch 3; repeat from ★ across, sc in top of turning ch: 7 ch-3 sps.

Row 4: Ch 4, turn; dc in first ch-3 sp, ch 1, ★ 4 dc in next ch-3 sp, ch 1, dc in next ch-3 sp, ch 1; repeat from ★ across, dc in last sc: 18 sts.

Row 5: Ch 1, turn; sc in first dc, ch 3, skip first ch-1 sp, sc in next ch-1 sp, ★ ch 3, sc in next ch-1 sp; repeat from ★ across to last sp, ch 3, skip next dc and next ch, sc in next ch: 7 ch-3 sps.

Repeat Rows 2-5 for pattern.

15. TREBLE CABLES
(Multiple of 12 + 4 chs)

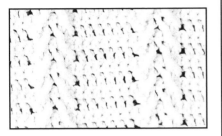

Ch 28 **loosely**.

Row 1 (Right side)**:** Dc in fourth ch from hook and in next 2 chs, † skip next ch, dc in next 2 chs, working in **front** of last 2 dc made, dc in skipped ch, skip next 2 chs, dc in next ch, working **behind** last dc made, dc in each of the 2 skipped chs †, dc in next 6 chs, repeat from † to † once, dc in last 4 chs: 26 sts.

Row 2: Ch 1, turn; sc in each st across.

To work Front Post Treble Crochet *(abbreviated FPtr)*, YO twice, insert hook from **front** to **back** around post of st indicated *(Fig. 1, page 20)*, YO and pull up a loop (4 loops on hook), (YO and draw through 2 loops on hook) 3 times.

Row 3: Ch 3 **(counts as first dc)**, turn; dc in next 3 sc, † skip next sc, dc in next 2 sc, working in **front** of last 2 dc made, work FPtr around post of dc one row **below** skipped sc, skip next 2 sc, work FPtr around post of dc **below** next sc, working **behind** last FPtr made, dc in each of 2 skipped sc, skip next sc †, dc in next 6 sc, repeat from † to † once, dc in last 4 sc.
Repeat Rows 2 and 3 for pattern.

---

16. ALTERNATE STITCH
(Multiple of 2 + 1 ch)

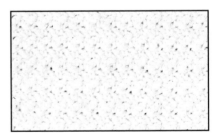

Ch 29 **loosely**.

Row 1: Sc in second ch from hook and in each ch across: 28 sc.

Row 2 (Right side)**:** Ch 1, turn; skip first sc, (sc, dc) in next sc, ★ skip next sc, (sc, dc) in next sc; repeat from ★ across.

Row 3: Ch 1, turn; (sc, dc) in each dc across.
Repeat Row 3 for pattern.

17. SHELLS & CORDS
(Multiple of 7 + 2 chs)

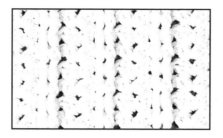

Ch 30 **loosely**.

Row 1: (2 Dc, ch 2, 2 dc) in sixth ch from hook, ★ skip next 2 chs, dc in next 2 chs, skip next 2 chs, (2 dc, ch 2, 2 dc) in next ch; repeat from ★ across to last 3 chs, skip next 2 chs, dc in last ch.

To work Front Post Double Crochet (abbreviated FPdc), YO, insert hook from **front** to **back** around post of st indicated **(Fig. 1, page 20)**, YO and pull up a loop (3 loops on hook), (YO and draw through 2 loops on hook) twice.

Row 2 (Right side)**:** Ch 3, turn; (2 dc, ch 2, 2 dc) in first ch-2 sp, skip next 2 dc, ★ work FPdc around post of next 2 dc, (2 dc, ch 2, 2 dc) in next ch-2 sp, skip next 2 dc; repeat from ★ across, dc in top of turning ch.

To work Back Post Double Crochet (abbreviated BPdc), YO, insert hook from **back** to **front** around post of st indicated **(Fig. 1, page 20)**, YO and pull up a loop (3 loops on hook), (YO and draw through 2 loops on hook) twice.

Row 3: Ch 3, turn; (2 dc, ch 2, 2 dc) in first ch-2 sp, ★ work BPdc around post of next 2 FPdc, (2 dc, ch 2, 2 dc) in next ch-2 sp; repeat from ★ across to last 3 sts, skip next 2 dc, dc in top of turning ch.

Row 4: Ch 3, turn; (2 dc, ch 2, 2 dc) in first ch-2 sp, ★ work FPdc around post of next 2 BPdc, (2 dc, ch 2, 2 dc) in next ch-2 sp; repeat from ★ across to last 3 sts, skip next 2 dc, dc in top of turning ch.

Repeat Rows 3 and 4 for pattern.

Last Row: Ch 2, turn; hdc in next dc, sc in next dc and in next ch-2 sp, sc in next dc, hdc in next dc, ★ (YO, insert hook in **next** st, YO and pull up a loop, YO and draw through 2 loops on hook) twice, YO and draw through all 3 loops on hook, hdc in next dc, sc in next dc and in next ch-2 sp, sc in next dc, hdc in next dc; repeat from ★ across to last st, hdc in top of turning ch; finish off.

18. FLYING SHELL
(Multiple of 4 + 2 chs)

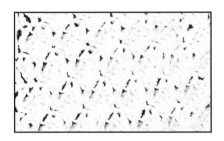

Ch 26 **loosely**.

Row 1 (Right side)**:** (Sc, ch 3, 3 dc) in second ch from hook, ★ skip next 3 chs, (sc, ch 3, 3 dc) in next ch; repeat from ★ across to last 4 chs, skip next 3 chs, sc in last ch.

Row 2: Ch 3, turn; dc in first sc, skip next 3 dc, sc in top of next ch-3, ★ (dc, ch 1, dc) in next sc, skip next 3 dc, sc in top of next ch-3; repeat from ★ across to last sc, 2 dc in last sc.

Row 3: Ch 3, turn; 3 dc in first dc, skip next dc, (sc, ch 3, 3 dc) in next sc, ★ skip next 2 dc, (sc, ch 3, 3 dc) in next sc; repeat from ★ across to last 5 sts, skip next 2 dc, sc in next sc, ch 3, YO, insert hook in next dc, YO and pull up a loop, YO and draw through 2 loops on hook, YO, insert hook in top of turning ch, YO and pull up a loop, YO and draw through 2 loops on hook, YO and draw through all 3 loops on hook.

Row 4: Ch 1, turn; sc in first st, ★ (dc, ch 1, dc) in next sc, skip next 3 dc, sc in top of next ch-3; repeat from ★ across.

Row 5: Ch 1, turn; (sc, ch 3, 3 dc) in first sc, ★ skip next 2 dc, (sc, ch 3, 3 dc) in next sc; repeat from ★ across to last 3 sts, skip next 2 dc, sc in last sc.
Repeat Rows 2-5 for pattern.

---

19. HDC PUFFS
(Multiple of 2 + 1 ch)

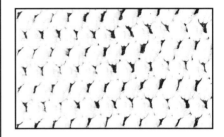

Ch 27 **loosely**.

To work Puff, ★ YO, insert hook in st indicated, YO and pull up a loop; repeat from ★ 2 times **more**, YO and draw through all 7 loops on hook.

Row 1 (Right side)**:** Work Puff in fifth ch from hook, ★ ch 1, skip next ch, work Puff in next ch; repeat from ★ across: 12 Puffs.

Row 2: Ch 3, turn; work Puff in first ch-1 sp, ch 1, ★ work Puff in next ch-1 sp, ch 1; repeat from ★ across, work Puff in sp of turning ch.
Repeat Row 2 for pattern.

20. PICOT BRICKS
(Multiple of 10 + 7 chs)

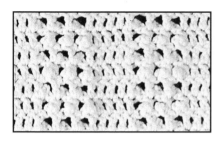

Ch 27 **loosely**.
To work Picot, ch 3, slip st in third ch from hook.
Row 1 (Right side): Dc in fourth ch from hook and in next 3 chs, ★ work Picot, skip next ch, (dc in next ch, work Picot, skip next ch) twice, dc in next 5 chs; repeat from ★ across.
Row 2: Ch 3 **(counts as first dc)**, turn; dc in next 4 dc, ★ work Picot, (dc in next dc, work Picot) twice, dc in next 5 dc; repeat from ★ across.
Repeat Row 2 for pattern.
Last Row: Ch 3, turn; dc in next 4 dc, ★ ch 1, (dc in next dc, ch 1) twice, dc in next 5 dc; repeat from ★ across; finish off.

21. FANS & CLUSTERS
(Multiple of 9 + 1 ch)

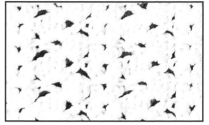

Ch 28 **loosely**.
To work Cluster, ★ YO, insert hook in st or sp indicated, YO and pull up a loop, YO and draw through 2 loops on hook; repeat from ★ once **more**, YO and draw through all 3 loops on hook.
Row 1 (Right side): Work (Cluster, ch 1, Cluster) in seventh ch from hook, ★ skip next 2 chs, (4 dc, ch 1, dc) in next ch, skip next 5 chs, work (Cluster, ch 1, Cluster) in next ch; repeat from ★ across to last 3 chs, ch 1, skip next 2 chs, dc in last ch.
Row 2: Ch 4, turn; skip first ch-1 sp, work (Cluster, ch 1, Cluster) in next ch-1 sp, ★ (4 dc, ch 1, dc) in next ch-1 sp, work (Cluster, ch 1, Cluster) in next ch-1 sp; repeat from ★ across, ch 1, skip next ch, dc in next ch.
Repeat Row 2 for pattern.

22. PUFF SHELLS
(Multiple of 9 + 2 chs)

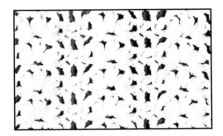

Ch 29 **loosely**.

Row 1 (Right side)**:** Sc in second ch from hook and in next ch, ch 1, skip next ch, sc in next ch, ch 3, skip next 2 chs, sc in next ch, ★ (ch 1, skip next ch, sc in next ch) 3 times, ch 3, skip next 2 chs, sc in next ch; repeat from ★ across to last 3 chs, ch 1, skip next ch, sc in last 2 chs.

To work Puff, ★ YO, insert hook in sp indicated, YO and pull up a loop; repeat from ★ 2 times **more**, YO and draw through all 7 loops on hook.

Row 2: Ch 1, turn; sc in first 2 sc, ch 1, work Puff in next ch-3 sp, (ch 3, work Puff in same sp) twice, ch 2, skip next sc, sc in next sc, ★ ch 1, sc in next sc, ch 1, work Puff in next ch-3 sp, (ch 3, work Puff in same sp) twice, ch 2, skip next sc, sc in next sc; repeat from ★ across to last sc, sc in last sc.

Row 3: Ch 3 **(counts as first dc, now and throughout)**, turn; dc in next sc, ch 1, sc in next ch-3 sp, ch 3, sc in next ch-3 sp, ★ ch 1, (dc in next sc, ch 1) twice, sc in next ch-3 sp, ch 3, sc in next ch-3 sp; repeat from ★ across to last 2 sc, ch 1, dc in last 2 sc.

Row 4: Ch 1, turn; sc in first 2 dc, ch 1, work Puff in next ch-3 sp, (ch 3, work Puff in same sp) twice, ch 2, ★ (sc in next dc, ch 1) twice, work Puff in next ch-3 sp, (ch 3, work Puff in same sp) twice, ch 2; repeat from ★ across to last 2 dc, sc in last 2 dc.

Repeat Rows 3 and 4 for pattern.

---

23. EXCHANGE STITCH
(Multiple of 2 chs)

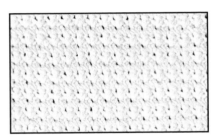

Ch 34 **loosely**.

Row 1: Sc in second ch from hook and in each ch across: 33 sc.

Row 2 (Right side)**:** Ch 1, turn; sc in first sc, ★ skip next sc, sc in next sc, working around sc just made, sc in skipped sc; repeat from ★ across.

Repeat Row 2 for pattern.

24. CLUSTERS & CROSSES
(Multiple of 5 + 3 chs)

Ch 28 **loosely**.

To work Cluster, ★ YO, insert hook in st or sp indicated, YO and pull up a loop, YO and draw through 2 loops on hook; repeat from ★ 2 times **more**, YO and draw through all 4 loops on hook.

Row 1 (Right side)**:** Work Cluster in sixth ch from hook, ★ ch 1, skip next 2 chs, dc in next ch, working in **front** of last dc made, dc in second skipped ch, ch 1, skip next ch, work Cluster in next ch; repeat from ★ across to last 2 chs, ch 1, skip next ch, dc in last ch: 5 Clusters.

Row 2: Ch 4, turn; skip first ch-1 sp, dc in next ch-1 sp, working in **front** of last dc made, dc in skipped ch-1 sp, ★ ch 1, work Cluster in sp **between** next 2 dc *(Fig. 2, page 20)*, ch 1, skip next ch-1 sp, dc in next ch-1 sp, dc in skipped ch-1 sp; repeat from ★ across, ch 1, dc in third ch of turning ch: 4 Clusters.

Row 3: Ch 4, turn; work Cluster in sp **between** next 2 dc, ch 1, ★ skip next ch-1 sp, dc in next ch-1 sp, working in **front** of last dc made, dc in skipped ch-1 sp, ch 1, work Cluster in sp **between** next 2 dc, ch 1; repeat from ★ across, dc in third ch of turning ch: 5 Clusters.

Repeat Rows 2 and 3 for pattern.

---

25. CRUNCH STITCH
(Multiple of 2 + 1 ch)

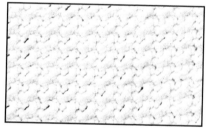

Ch 25 **loosely**.

Row 1: Slip st **loosely** in third ch from hook, (hdc in next ch, slip st **loosely** in next ch) across.

Row 2 (Right side)**:** Ch 2, turn; skip first slip st, (slip st **loosely** in next hdc, hdc in next slip st) across to last st, slip st **loosely** in top of turning ch.

Repeat Row 2 for pattern.

26. GARDEN ROWS
(Multiple of 10 + 7 chs)

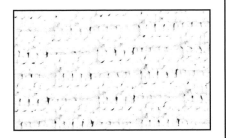

Ch 27 **loosely**.

Row 1 (Right side)**:** Dc in fourth ch from hook and in each ch across: 25 sts.

To work Front Post Single Crochet *(abbreviated FPsc),* insert hook from **front** to **back** around post of st indicated *(Fig. 1, page 20),* YO and pull up a loop, YO and draw through both loops on hook. Skip st behind FPsc.

Row 2: Ch 1, turn; work FPsc around first 5 dc, ★ dc in next dc, (sc in next dc, dc in next dc) twice, work FPsc around next 5 dc; repeat from ★ across.

Row 3: Ch 3 **(counts as first dc, now and throughout)**, turn; dc in next st and in each st across.

Row 4: Ch 1, turn; sc in first 2 dc, dc in next dc, sc in next dc, dc in next dc, work FPsc around next 5 dc, dc in next dc, (sc in next dc, dc in next dc) twice, work FPsc around next 5 dc, dc in next dc, sc in next dc, dc in next dc, sc in last 2 dc.

Row 5: Ch 3, turn; dc in next st and in each st across.

Repeat Rows 2-5 for pattern.

---

27. LEAF STITCH
(Multiple of 2 + 1 ch)

Ch 31 **loosely**.

Row 1: Sc in second ch from hook and in each ch across: 30 sc.

Row 2 (Right side)**:** Ch 1, turn; skip first sc, 2 sc in next sc, ★ skip next sc, 2 sc in next sc; repeat from ★ across.

Repeat Row 2 for pattern.

28. HERRINGBONE
(Multiple of 12 + 4 chs)

Ch 28 **loosely**.

Row 1 (Right side)**:** Sc in second ch from hook, ★ ch 1, skip next ch, sc in next ch; repeat from ★ across: 14 sc.

Row 2: Ch 1, turn; sc in first sc, ★ ch 1, sc in next sc; repeat from ★ across.

Row 3: Ch 1, turn; sc in first sc, ch 1, sc in next sc, ★ ch 6, skip next 2 ch-1 sps, slip st in skipped ch of beginning ch **below** next ch-1 sp, ch 6, skip next 2 ch-1 sps, sc in next sc, ch 1, sc in next sc; repeat from ★ across.

Row 4: Ch 1, turn; sc in first sc, ch 1, sc in next sc, ★ (ch 1, dc in next sc) 4 times, (ch 1, sc in next sc) twice; repeat from ★ across.

Row 5: Ch 1, turn; sc in first sc, ch 1, sc in next sc, ★ ch 6, slip st in skipped ch one row **above** previous slip st, ch 6, sc in next sc, ch 1, sc in next sc; repeat from ★ across.

Row 6: Ch 1, turn; sc in first sc, ch 1, sc in next sc, ★ (ch 1, dc in next dc) 4 times, (ch 1, sc in next sc) twice; repeat from ★ across.

Repeat Rows 5 and 6 for pattern, ending by working Row 5.

Next Row: Ch 1, turn; sc in first sc, ch 1, sc in next sc, ★ (ch 1, sc in next dc) 4 times, (ch 1, sc in next sc) twice; repeat from ★ across.

Next Row: Ch 1, turn; sc in first sc, ch 1, sc in next sc, ★ ch 6, slip st in skipped ch one row **above** previous slip st, ch 6, skip next 4 sc of previous row, sc in next sc, ch 1, sc in next sc; repeat from ★ across.

Last 2 Rows: Ch 1, turn; sc in first sc, (ch 1, sc in next sc) across; finish off.

29. HONEYCOMB
(Multiple of 3 + 2 chs)

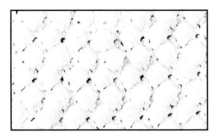

Ch 26 **loosely**.
Row 1: Sc in second ch from hook and in each ch across: 25 sc.
To work Cluster, ★ YO, insert hook in sc indicated, YO and pull up a loop, YO and draw through 2 loops on hook; repeat from ★ 4 times **more**, YO and draw through all 6 loops on hook, pushing Cluster to **right** side if necessary.
Row 2 (Right side)**:** Ch 1, turn; sc in first sc, ★ work Cluster in next sc, sc in next 2 sc; repeat from ★ across: 8 Clusters.
Row 3: Ch 1, turn; sc in each st across: 25 sc.
Row 4: Ch 1, turn; sc in first 2 sc, work Cluster in next sc, ★ sc in next 2 sc, work Cluster in next sc; repeat from ★ across to last sc, sc in last sc: 8 Clusters.
Row 5: Ch 1, turn; sc in each st across: 25 sc.
Repeat Rows 2-5 for pattern.

30. SWEET PEA
(Multiple of 7 chs)

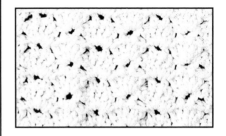

Ch 28 **loosely**.
Row 1 (Right side)**:** Dc in fourth ch from hook, ★ skip next 2 chs, 5 dc in next ch (5-dc group), skip next 2 chs, dc in next 2 chs (2-dc group); repeat from ★ across to last 3 chs, skip next 2 chs, 3 dc in last ch.
Row 2: Ch 3, turn; dc in sp **between** first 2 dc *(Fig. 2, page 20)*, ★ 5 dc in sp **between** dc of next 2-dc group, dc in sp **between** second and third dc of next 5-dc group and in next sp **(between** third and fourth dc); repeat from ★ across to last 4 sts, 3 dc in sp **between** last dc and turning ch.
Repeat Row 2 for pattern.

GENERAL INSTRUCTIONS

ABBREVIATIONS

BPdc	Back Post double crochet(s)
ch(s)	chain(s)
dc	double crochet(s)
FPdc	Front Post double crochet(s)
FPsc	Front Post single crochet(s)
FPtr	Front Post treble crochet(s)
hdc	half double crochet(s)
sc	single crochet(s)
sp(s)	space(s)
st(s)	stitch(es)
tr	treble crochet(s)
YO	yarn over

★ — work instructions following ★ as many **more** times as indicated in addition to the first time.

† to † — work all instructions from first † to second † **as many** times as specified.

( ) — work enclosed instructions **as many** times as specified by the number immediately following **or** work all enclosed instructions in the stitch or space indicated **or** contains explanatory remarks.

colon (:) — the number(s) given after a colon at the end of a row or round denote(s) the number of stitches or spaces you should have on that row or round.

MULTIPLES

The multiple for each pattern stitch is listed below the ID Photo. The multiple indicates the number of chains required to form one complete pattern of the design.

Different pattern stitches produce a different number of stitches and/or rows per inch with the same yarn and the same size hook. Therefore, patterns which share the same multiple will not necessarily be interchangeable, because each may produce a different gauge.

GAUGE

Gauge refers to the number of stitches and rows in a given area. The size of a stitch will vary depending on the yarn, the size of your hook, and the way you control the yarn. In the Pattern Stitch section, there is no gauge or hook size specified because each pattern can be worked in your choice of yarn to vary the size and appearance of the design.

YARN

Before choosing the yarn and hooks for your project, you may want to experiment with a variety of weights until you achieve the appearance and texture that you desire. Yarn weight (type or size) is divided into six basic categories:

Fingering: Fine weight yarns that make great socks and beautiful baby clothes.

Sport: Most often used for lightweight sweaters, baby clothes, and baby afghans.

Double Knit: Most often used for sweaters and afghans.

Worsted: Makes great sweaters, vests, and afghans.

Heavy Worsted: Most often used for heavy sweaters and afghans.

Bulky: Generally used to make heavy sweaters, jackets, and coats.

POST STITCH

Work around post of stitch indicated, inserting hook in direction of arrow *(Fig. 1)*.

Fig. 1

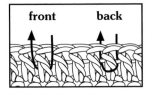

WORKING IN SPACE BEFORE A STITCH

When instructed to work in space **before** a stitch or in space **between** stitches, insert hook in space indicated by arrow *(Fig. 2)*.

Fig. 2

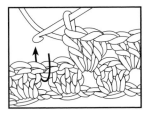

BASIC STITCHES

CHAIN

To work a chain stitch, begin with a slip knot on the hook. Bring the yarn **over** hook from back to front, catching the yarn with the hook and turning the hook slightly toward you to keep the yarn from slipping off. Draw the yarn through the slip knot *(Fig. 3)* **(first chain st made,** *abbreviated ch)*.

Fig. 3

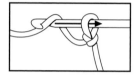

WORKING INTO THE CHAIN

When counting chains, always begin with the first chain from the hook and then count toward the beginning of your foundation chain *(Fig. 4a)*.

Fig. 4a

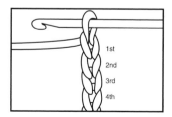

Method 1: Insert hook under top two strands of each chain *(Fig. 4b)*.

Fig. 4b

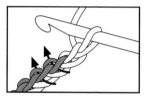

Method 2: Insert hook into back ridge of each chain *(Fig. 4c)*.

Fig. 4c

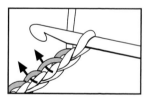

SLIP STITCH

To work a slip stitch, insert hook in st or sp indicated, YO and draw through st and through loop on hook *(Fig. 5)* **(slip stitch made,** *abbreviated slip st)*.

Fig. 5

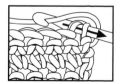